Do Not
Disturb
Any Further

DO NOT DISTURB ANY FURTHER

JOHN CALLAHAN

John Callahan is no ordinary cartoonist. Abandoned at birth by his mother, he was educated by Roman Catholic nuns with an emphasis on guilt and harsh discipline, he became an alcoholic by the age of 12 and was paralysed in a car accident shortly after his 21st birthday. It took six years of heavy drinking before Callahan got to realise that his problem was alcoholism and not quadriplegia. With his recovery, he returned to a childhood passion and started working hard on his cartoons. Callahan can't move all his fingers, so he draws by clutching a pen in his right hand and guiding it across the page with his left.

Now some fifteen years later, Callahan's work appears in over forty newspapers and his autobiography 'Don't worry, He won't get far on foot' has been published to critical and commercial success.

Published by Statics (London) Ltd
41 Standard Road, London NW10 6HF
Copyright © 1990 by John Callahan

Printed in England by H.P.H. Print Ltd.
8 Gorst Road, London NW10 6LE.

ISBN 1 - 873922 - 04 - 3

DO NOT DISTURB ANY FURTHER

JOHN CALLAHAN

STATICS BOOKS

CALLAHAN

"YOU'LL FIND WE DON'T STAND ON FORMALITY AROUND HERE."

"LET'S HEAR FROM THAT DUMPY MAN WITH THE THICK GLASSES."

"IT'S JUST THAT I'VE NEVER HEARD OF A 'SPERM DRIVE' BEFORE."

"JUST WHEN I THOUGHT THINGS COULDN'T GET ANY WORSE!"

"YOU'RE A TRANSVESTITE, AREN'T YOU? I LIKE THAT IN A MAN!"

"BASICALLY, MR. WILSON, WHAT I SEEM TO BE HEARING YOU SAY IS 'HELP'!"

"DON'T BE A FOOL, BILLY!"

CALLAHAN

"YOU KIDS QUIT BOTHERING YOUR FATHER FOR MONEY!"

"HOW MUCH IS THAT WINDOW IN THE DOGGIE?"

"ALIEN HELL! I'M THE THIN PERSON TRYING TO GET OUT OF YOU!"

"I'M SO HOPING LITTLE SHERMAN WILL TURN OUT TO BE SOMETHING SUCCESSFUL: A DOCTOR, A LAWYER, A JAPANESE."

"I'LL HAVE MY PEOPLE CALL YOUR PEOPLE ABOUT LETTING MY PEOPLE GO."

"WELL, THAT'S A HELLUVA GODDAM NOTE! I WINE YOU, DINE YOU, BLOW FIFTY BUCKS ON FLOWERS AND TAXI FARE, AND NOW I FIND OUT YOU'RE CELIBATE!"

"MY TECHNIQUE FOR RECTAL EXAMINATION IS SOMEWHAT DIFFERENT IN THAT I'M GAY AND HAVE NO ARMS."

"WHAT'S HAPPENED TO OUR SEX LIFE, DARLING?"

"I NEED A HUG!"

"HAVE YOU CONSIDERED SOMETHING IN A SOLID COLOR?"

CALLAHAN

"I'D LIKE TO THANK ALL THOSE WHO MADE IT POSSIBLE FOR ME TO BE HERE TONIGHT."

"I'M FINALLY BEGINNING TO GET SOME ATTENTION FOR WHAT I HAVE
UPSTAIRS!"

"SOMEONE SAID HE WAS DEPRESSED ABOUT HIS CHOLESTEROL LEVEL."

"DON'T WORRY, HE WON'T GET FAR ON FOOT."

CALLAHAN

"OKAY, LET'S GET THOSE EYEBALLS MOVING!!"

"MISS GORDON, PLEASE LIVE MY LIFE FOR ME."

"DON'T YOU LOVE IT WHEN THEY'RE STILL WARM FROM THE DRYER?"

"WELL, YOU CAN STAY HOME FROM SCHOOL, BUT YOU'D BETTER BE POSSESSED!"

"YOU'RE GOING BACK TO THAT SURGEON AND DEMANDING A MORE
ATTRACTIVE PROSTHETIC DEVICE!"

"ALL THOSE WHO ENJOY MAKING PIRATE SOUNDS, SAY 'AYE!' ALL THOSE
WHO ENJOY MAKING HORSE SOUNDS, SAY 'NAY!'"

CALLAHAN

"SO . . . WHERE DO YOU GO FROM HERE?"

CALLAHAN

"EXCUSE ME, BUT I THINK THOSE SEATS HAVE ALREADY BEEN PISSED AROUND."

"YOU'RE NOT HERE, WILSON. I LIKE THAT IN AN EMPLOYEE."

"OF COURSE YOU'RE NOT FEELING WELL—YOU HAVEN'T THROWN UP A
THING ALL DAY!"

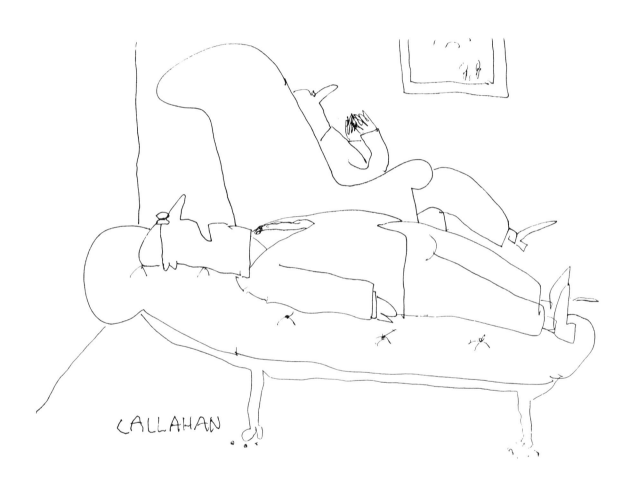

"I'D LIKE TO MASTURBATE, BUT I DON'T FEEL I DESERVE MYSELF."

"MOMMY! MOMMY! CAN WE KILL THE PUPPIES?!!"

"MISS ALLEN, PLEASE BRING ME A BAVARIAN CAP AND A FLUTE."

"I WAS HARSHLY TOILET TRAINED AS A CHILD."

"I AM NOW GOING TO HOLD MY BREATH UNTIL EVERYONE HAS TAKEN A
SEAT AND IS QUIETLY PAYING ATTENTION."

"PEOPLE LIKE YOU ARE A REAL INSPIRATION TO ME!"

"IT HURTS WHEN I GO LIKE THIS!"

CALLAHAN

"LET'S TALK A LITTLE ABOUT THOSE HALLUCINATIONS."

"OF COURSE THINGS AREN'T ALWAYS EASY—CHUCK BEING ON THE ROAD MOST OF THE TIME."